MW00511183

MACRAMÈ

THE NEW STEP BY STEP ILLUSTRATED
GUIDE TO MAKE YOUR HOME ELEGANT AND
REFINED. IMPRESS YOUR FRIENDS AND
FAMILY WITH GREAT GIFTS (HOW TO MAKE
PLANT HANGERS, PATTERNS, JEWELRY,
KNOTS AND MORE)

BY

ROSE SMITH

indirect, which are incurred as a result of the use of information contained within this document, including, but not limited to, — errors, omissions, or inaccuracies.

Table of Contents

INTRODUCTION

Macramé might be the millennial DIY existing apart from everything else, except it goes back hundreds of years! Macramé is all over! You don't need to search far for a workshop at a yoga studio devoted to telling you the best way to weave together a knotty wall hanging, a drapery plant hanger, or a little key chain. The mixes of boho and moderate make for a warm yet chic look. If you've as of late decorated your home with it, regardless of whether it was a DIY project (like the windy macramé room divider), or got a previously made piece at the swap meet or even TJ Maxx, your folks might be bewildered when they visit. How did this much-censured '70s relic find new life in the 21st century?

It couldn't be any more obvious, the thing about anything crawling once again from '70s style is that it was certifiably not an especially flourishing time for design. Whole rooms were committed to avocado green, from the rug to the walls to the bedding, with sprinkles of collect gold balancing it. Yuck! And keeping in mind that those hues can remain during the '70s, macramé is back, giving encouraging surface to white walls, and standing out high from precious green plants.

Macramé Defined

Macramé is a kind of textile made using knotting strategies, instead of weaving or sewing. The knots are square and structure full-hitch and twofold half-hitches. The craft required just modest and available materials like cotton twine, hemp, calfskin, or yarn, with different beads used to improve the piece. It's the craft of knotting string or harmony into ornamental or helpful things. There are loads of various knots to discover that will give you an alternate look and feel! Like any ability, macramé requires some serious energy, tolerance, and practice! When you get the hang of things, you'll be knotting up a wide range of cool and insane bits of artistry!

The main records of macramé are credited to thirteenth-century Arab weavers who utilized additional string to make knotted beautifying strings on handcrafted textures. Third-century China has additionally attributed gratitude to the skillet chang knot—a progression of circles that mesh into limitlessness images to speak to life span. Mariners are likewise a significant piece of the craft's beginnings in the Great Age of Sail, or the 1700s to around 1830, when they utilized the knots to stun up their blades, jugs, and parts of the boat, while their insight into various kinds of knots was utilized to deal Intel!

The '70s took the resplendent rope work standard when macramé turned into a well-known textile that transformed into decorations, placemats, and plant slings in the corner, picture outlines, loungers, wall hangings, and even two-pieces. While the fame burnt out after the '70s, a restored intrigue was as of late started in DIY instructional exercises on YouTube and bloggers' very own locales.

Condo tenants find macramé especially satisfying for its capacity to change the many hanging house plants all through their space as a response to the absence of a yard, and a methods for carrying the outside in with an ever-increasing number of structures springing up and trees being chopped down (you should look at this indoor hanging herb garden, as well). So whenever your folks wonder why you've gone macramé insane, you can gesture to the rich history of hundreds of years past for motivating your craft assault.

Macramé can be as essential as only a couple of basic knots to hold your indoor house plants, a happy improvement, a fishbowl, or whatever else you can think of! Or on the other hand, it very well may be more convoluted and turn into another bit of fine art on your wall. You can go through it to flavor an exhausting thing, or, to add a boho look to a couple of sandals, a headband or even a camera! When you get the hang of this new ability, you will knot up whatever your heart wants and adding macramé to the entirety of your stuff! Macramé is amusing to do and can be an incredible method to invest energy with companions as you tattle, drink tea, and macramé yourselves kinship bracelets!

Macramé—is one of the numerous crafts being restored by the individuals who love working with their hands. Much the same as surface weaving, stitching, and embroidery are seeing a knock in fame, macramé is being changed from a 1970s relic into a hot, stylish work of art.

A flexible type of fiber artistry, macramé can be utilized to make everything from wall hangings and plant hangers to gems, handbags, and in any event, clothing things. Using straightforward materials like cotton twine, jute, and hemp, or yarn, macramé can be as basic or intricate as the crafter might want. Additions like glass or wooden beads, just as colored strings, can likewise open up a scope of imaginative prospects. Become familiar with somewhat more about the captivating history of macramé before jumping into essential methods and counsel on the best way to begin making your own or buying some contemporary macramé.

Brief History of Macramé

Macramé filled each alcove and cranes during the 70s. Macramé's underlying foundations are quite fascinating, with a history going back a large number of years. Some accept that the term originates from the thirteenth-century Arabic word migramah, which signifies "periphery." Others take its inceptions to lie in the

Turkish word makrama, which alludes to "napkin" or "towel," and was an approach to make sure about bits of weaving by using overabundance strings along the top or base of woven textures. These enlivening edges were initially used to keep takes off creatures (camels and ponies) in the hot African desert locales.

In any case, improving macramé in reality first shows up in quite a while by the Babylonians and Assyrians that portray bordered plaiting used to embellish outfits. In the thirteenth century, Arab weavers utilized embellishing knots to complete the overabundance string on cloaks, shroud, and towels. It at that point spread to Europe through North Africa, when the Moors brought macramé to Spain.

While most consider macramé a rage of the 1970s, the craft arrived at top prominence in Victorian England. First acquainted with England in the late seventeenth century, Queen Mary herself instructed classes to her women in-pausing. Most Victorian homes had some sort of macramé enhancement, as it was utilized not exclusively to enliven clothing, yet additionally as curtains, decorative spreads, and quilts.

Given their expertise at making knots, it should not shock anyone that mariners are to a great extent, answerable for spreading macramé around the globe. It was an extraordinary method to relax and could then be traded or sold when they docked, in this manner carrying it to zones like China and the New World. Loungers, belts, and ringer borders were a portion of the great things made by British and American mariners in the nineteenth century. Writings like 1877's The Imperial Macramé Lace Book, which expounds on various knots and examples, show precisely how important the strategy was at that point.

In the wake of blurring in ubiquity, macramé saw a resurgence during the 1970s. It came to represent the Bohemian style and was utilized to make wall hangings, plant hangers, embellishments, and clothing. The craft in the end melted away in fame; however, slants will, in general, be much patterned. Presently, macramé is back, making waves again as inventive crafters concoct contemporary examples that have renewed the noteworthy knotting strategies.

How did macramé spread over the world?

During long inaccessible excursions, mariners made macramé and sold or bargained when they landed. Not a fascinating history. However, particularly as the rage for macramé blurred. In the mid-70s, it recovered prominence, and this time served better for wall hangings, cover, decorative liner, draperies, and so forth. By the mid-80s macramé had dropped out of style as an improvement pattern and blurred. Macramé was generally well known in the Victorian period. Sylvia's Book of Macramé Lace

(1882), a top pick, indicated peruses how "to work luxurious trimmings for dark and hued ensembles, both for home wear, garden parties, ocean side ramblings, and balls—fairylike embellishments for the family unit and underlines... "

Present-day Macramé Styles—basic and great!

Check out today, this pattern is returning, and this time it's not constrained to quilts, draperies, or decorative liner. Presently it incorporates crystal fixtures and adornments with a mix of different globules (glass, stone, or wood), pendants or shells, and more thoughts popping each day.

Macramé for Beginners

Much the same as anything in life, there is a constant number of approaches to learning another expertise or craft. I won't profess to be a specialist on macramé. I am an absolute beginner. Starting with one beginner then onto the next, I am mainly going to take you through my excursion to give you one approach to do it.

I will give all the assets you have to locate your specific manner to grasp the excellent craft of macramé. The cool part is that you don't should be a specialist to make completely beautiful stylistic theme pieces for you home. Indeed, it looks a lot harder than it is. Thus, how about we get to it.

The Most Effective Method to Do Macramé

It isn't too advisable for you to rehearse first? Like most projects, this is going to cost you a few bucks. What amount? Indeed, my first 'genuine' project cost me about $30 for the macramé rope (or macramé line, as it is in some cases alluded to) and two or three dollars for the wooden dowel. Also, you can't get down to Hobby Lobby or Michael's and purchase the macramé rope or macramé rope. You will need to arrange it (more on that later). In this way, in case you're similar to me, and you like to begin a project the day you at long last say to yourself, "I need to begin this" my recommendation is to start as I did with a training project.

Macramé Practice Project

Reasons I suggest a little "practice" project:

• It occupies the delay while you sit tight for your macramé rope.

• This will help you become acquainted with various macramé knots, their names, and how to do them.

- By the finish of your training project, you'll either be extremely cheerful and entirely eager for more significant outputs, or you'll understand this simply isn't for you.

- Completing this training project will give you the certainty to put away your time and cash to make the next move to your first "genuine" macramé project.

What kinds of macramé projects would I be able to make? Start little.

- Plant holder

- Jewelry including choker necklaces or bracelets

- Wall-hanging

- Bookmark

- Key chain

- Bigger projects include:

- Table sprinter

• Hammock (spare a significant project like this for some other time)

• Light installation

• Rug

• Headboard

• Garland or hitting

Settle on the project type. Plant holders and Wall hangings are the two well-known starter projects.

Where is it going to go? This will help figure out what size you're hoping to make. Discover a style that interests you. All the more freestyle and natural or symmetric with clean lines and adequately characterized designs?

What Materials Do I Need for Macramé?

When you have your project/design, you will realize how much rope to purchase. I realized I needed to utilize normal cotton rope; however, you can allow your own to taste and style direct you as you pick your shading and material. They sell cable (or line) on Etsy. Be that as it may, it wasn't accessible in the sum or value I needed. After a great deal of looking, here is the connection I utilized.

Here is a rundown of the considerable number of materials you will require:

- Cotton macramé string (rope)

- Wood or metal dowel, or equal tree limb or debris (for an increasingly natural characteristic look), in case you're doing wall craftsmanship

- Hanging ring if making a plant hanger

- Scissors

- Tape measure

- Tape (I utilized painters' tape which was anything but difficult to expel, however veiling tape would likewise be excellent)

- If you would prefer not to utilize tape, you could "seal" the finishes by softening the closures with a light fire as an alternative.

- Rolling rack for garments (or elective strategy for the hanging project, see beneath)

The amount Time my Large Macramé Project will take

This relies to a great extent upon the project that you pick, yet for mine, the genuine work took around more than two hours. Altogether, it took me about three hours since I was looking into the knots by viewing YouTube recordings.

Would I be able to do this?

Indeed, I'm here to reveal to you that you can.

How frequently long does it take to learn a Macramé Knot? On my training project, I forgot about how often I needed to rewind the video to the start and begin once again. Furthermore, indeed, I had minutes when I thought about whether this was true for me. In this way, it's ordinary to have passing questions along your expectation to absorb information. Do not let this stop you from achieving your aim. You might not "get" the knot until your tenth time. Be that as it may, you will get it. Simply continue stopping endlessly. Your second is practically around the bend.

DIY Project Made Easy Hints

Clue No. 1: On my first project, I never truly got the "corner to corner clove hitch knot." No issue what I attempted, it never resembled the video. I tore out the whole line a few times and began once again around multiple times. I, at long last, chose to "let it go." I speculated that the little string I was working with didn't loan itself well to this line. It only wasn't going to appear to be identical.

Furthermore, prepare to have your mind blown. I was correct. When I began working with the bigger rope, the askew clove hitch knot looked precisely like the image. What's the exercise here? Try not to surrender, my companions.

Clue No. 2: The first occasion when I investigated the example, it seemed as though I was perusing a page of Chinese. No compelling reason to freeze. Recollect what I said? You can do this. Do what I did. Approach it slowly and carefully. That is how you will endure this. It's not hard if you make it stride by step and monitor which step you are on. My one slip-up I made (I needed to tear out a whole column) I made because I got excessively loose and didn't give enough consideration to the bit by bit process.

Tip: To monitor where you are in the means, I suggest using a highlighter and separating the ways as you complete them.

Strategic Macramé Questions Answered:

Could macramé be washed? Truly. Macramé is durable and doesn't fall apart without any problem. It very well may be machine washed at 86 degrees F in a little suitcase. Hang to dry.

Would you be able to utilize yarn to macramé? Truly. You can utilize yarn. You should simply comprehend that the size of the macramé knots might be as large as the yarn or material that you use. The littler the string, yarn or rope you pick, the littler the knots will be. If the yarn is too little, the knots won't be truly obvious. Yarn may be a material most appropriate to a smaller scale macramé project for use in adornments making, for instance, instead of for a more significant project like a wall hanging.

Would you be able to macramé with jute? Truly. Jute and hemp used to be extremely mainstream with macramé artisans; however, their absence of accessibility in the market offered to ascend to using macramé strings out of nylon and glossy silk rayon and other human-made filaments. For tenderfoots, cotton or nylon ropes are prescribed because they are simpler to unwind on account of a misstep.

How would I pick what kind of macramé line to use for my project? There are numerous interesting points while picking your material. Accessibility and cost is continually something clear to consider. In any case, you may likewise need to think about the quality of the material for your project. If you need to hang a plant, for instance, you need to pick a more grounded line like those made out of jute, calfskin, strip, nylon, or cotton.

Likewise, you ought to think about the firmness of the string. For adornments, you will need to utilize more slender, progressively adaptable lines like weaving rope, which is made of cotton and is delicate and adaptable. If doing an outside project, either an open-air plant holder or open-air lounger, you might need to pick a polypropylene rope that is strong and depended.

What size string would it be advisable for me to utilize? Contingent upon your project, you will need to pick a thickness of 4.0 mm in the distance across or more for more significant improvements like wall hangings or plant holders. For littler smaller scale macramé projects like bracelets and necklaces, you ought to pick string that is under 2.0 mm in breadth.

What amount of line do I require for macramé? The strings that you will use for knotting should be around five to multiple times the completed length. The ropes that are your "center" ropes that are being utilized for the shape yet not being knotted may just be about double the completed length. Make sure to leave additional line length for making periphery or other beautifying options at the closures. What's more, it's smarter to have an excessive amount of rope than pretty much nothing. You can generally trim long pieces toward the end.

How would I keep my knots looking uniform? The ideal approach to ensure that your knots are costume is to ensure that you keep the strain on your ropes even and that each knot lines up straight on all sides, on a level plane, vertically, and corner to corner. Particularly when you are merely learning, you will need to check each knot and ensure that it lines up with the procedure knot that the edges are firm and the circles are even. The ideal approach to safeguard that your project turns out also is to make sure about your project. For more significant projects, you will need to balance them from a garments rack or a safe snare. Preferably you will drape your project from two focuses with the goal that the project doesn't swing to and fro. For littler projects like gems, you will need to make a macramé board.

What is a macramé board?

A macramé board is where you will make sure about your project for knotting. This can be made out of a wide range of materials, yet essentially you need to make a firm surface that you can embed pins into. You can utilize a plugboard, a bit of polyurethane, or two bits of cardboard associated together. The board ought to be around 12 inches square and thick enough to embed a T pin or corsage pin into without standing out the opposite side.

Why is macramé making a reflection?

Macramé was well known, harking back to the 1970s with the nonconformist culture. However, it has returned into style as a feature of the ongoing ancestral and Boho (Bohemian) design patterns in the home stylistic theme.

Macramé Art

I'm sure you have gone over with a beautiful macramé wall hanging or a comfortable plant hanger. The bohemian impact joined with the moderation of macramé craft makes a warm yet chic look. If you are interested in how it functions, simply continue perusing! Macramé is a French word that implies knot, and it is the craft of interfacing enhancing knots. Assyrians and Persians began rehearsing macramé knots and carried it to expressive arts level. At that point, it is acquainted with Europeans by Arabs and Europeans took it to the Americas.

Macramé Cords

Macramé is finished by hand, and you don't have to utilize any weaving needles or sew snares, and macramé designs are much simpler than they hope to follow. The yarn you use for macramé is called macramé string. You can utilize different materials, for example, cotton twine, hemp, cowhide, or yarn, you can even include different beads for an alternate vibe. The most significant moment that picking which material to use for a project is to consider what the completed thing is and how it will be utilized. For specific projects, thick and durable macramé rope will be better, and for some others, using fine and delicate macramé yarn will be progressively usable. In the model, the XX Lace Yarn is immaculate to make a reliable plant hanger or a shopping bag, while the Macramé Cake is flawless to cause a gentler to feel classy sprinter with its smooth shading changes!

Macramé Knots

To breathe life into a macramé design, just thing you have to learn is only a few fundamental macramé knots. Do you extravagant a bohemian macramé shade? What about a boho and chic macramé decorative linen? It's simple peasy lemon squeezy! The initial two terms you have to learn is knotting line (the string or set of tracks that is utilized to make the knot for some random line) and knot bearing string (the string or set of ropes that the knotting lines are folded over). The most widely recognized and essential macramé knots are "half a knot, square knot, vertical half-hitch, and slanting half-hitch." You can finish a wide range of macramé projects with just these four knots.

The most effective method to Macramé: Basic Knots to Master

Macramé has been a well-known approach to brighten for quite a long time, bringing surface and warmth into a home with knots that can be assembled in one of a kind methods to make unique wall hangings, plant holders, and the sky is the limit from there. It's anything but difficult to figure out how to macramé since you just need to know a bunch of knots to make a macramé project.

Getting Reading to Knot - Before you're prepared to begin figuring out how to macramé, assemble your provisions, and acquaint yourself with some regular macramé terms you'll have to know.

Supplies and Materials

This is what you'll have to realize and rehearse your macramé knots:

- Macramé Cord: This can be just about any sort of string, twine, or rope made out of cotton, hemp, jute, or manufactured material. It comes in various sizes, hues, and winds. In this instructional exercise, we utilized a 3/16" cotton line sold as rope for clotheslines.

- Support: You'll need something to attach your knots to. Well-known decisions incorporate dowel bars, branches, loops, or rings. We utilized a dowel pole for these knots.

- Scissors

Significant Macramé Terms

There are a couple of significant macramé terms you'll have to know before you can begin.

- Working Cord: The rope or set of ropes that you use to make the natural knots.

- Filler Cord: The string or set of ropes that your knots fold over.

- Sennit: A set of knots or knot that are worked in repeat.

Lark's Head Knot

The first knot you'll have to know is the Lark's Head Knot, now and then alluded to as a Cow Hitch Knot. This knot is the thing that gets your macramé strings appended to an article, for example, dowel, branch, or a stay string.

Crease your rope fifty-fifty and spot the circle over the dowel bar.

Bring the circle around the back and get your two-line closes through the loop to fix.

Reverse Lark's Head Knot

The Reverse Lark's Knot is done in the reverse direction, so the knock is covered up in the rear of the knot.

Overlay the line into equal parts and spot the circle under the dowel bar.

A circle under a dowel pole

Bring the circle round to the front and get your two ropes through the loop to fix.

Square Knots & Half Knots

Square knot is one of the most generally utilized macramé knots, and it very well may be made as left confronting or right confronting.

A half knot is essentially 50% of a square knot. It very well may be correct confronting or left confronting, contingent upon which side you start on.

Square knots need to have at any rate four ropes (2 working ropes and two filler lines) yet can have more. The first and last strings are the working lines. We'll call them working chain 1 and 4. The center lines are filler strings, and we'll number those 2 and 3. These lines will switch puts; however, will even now keep their unique numbering.

Left Facing Half Knot and Square Knot

A left confronting square knot has a vertical knock on the left half of the completed knot.

Take the main string (working string 1) and move it to the director over the center filler ropes (filler ropes 2 and 3) and under the last string (working string 4).

Line 1 over lines 2 and 3 however under string 4

Take working line 4 and move it to one side under the two filler ropes and overworking string 1.

Line 4 under filler lines and over line 1

Pull both working lines to fix, keeping the filler lines straight. This is a left confronting half square knot.

Fixing the left confronting square half knot

The working lines have now exchanged spots with working line 1 on the privilege and working string four on the left. Take working rope one and move it to one side over the two filler ropes and underworking line 4.

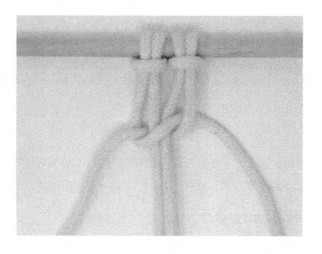

Rope 1 going over the filler ropes and under rope 4

Take working rope four and move it to one side under the two filler strings and overworking rope 1.

CHAPTER ONE

PROJECT ONE: MACRAMÉ FEATHERS

Excellent, wispy macramé feathers have been obstructing the online life takes care of starting late - however, I'm not distraught about it. They're unbelievably attractive, and I've certainly gotten myself bookmarking them to buy later, to hang in the children's room. I was likewise interested to know how they were made. How on the planet do you accomplish that altogether delicate periphery?! I later found all of the solutions needed. Furthermore, it includes a feline brush. That's all anyone needs to know. Indeed, the conceivable outcomes are tremendous here, and I realize you can hardly wait to mess with this strategy more. However, meanwhile, I trust I'll move you to make these at home. These in vogue boho feathers are an astounding novice macramé project for you to have a ton of fun creating with companions!

You'll need:

*   5mm single curve cotton string

*   Fabric stiffener

- Sharp texture shears

- Cat brush

- Ruler

For a medium measured feather, cut:

- 1 32" strand for the spine

- 10-12 14" strands for the top

- 8-10 12" strands for the center

- 6-8 10" strands for the base

Overlap the 32" strand fifty-fifty. Take one of the 14" strands, crease it into equal parts and fold it under the spine.

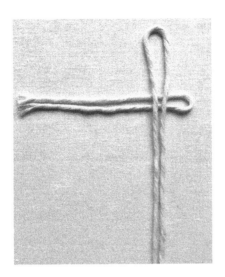

Presently pull the base strands entirely through the top circle. This is your knot!

Pull the two sides firmly. On the following line, you'll interchange the beginning side so if you laid the flat strand from left to right the first occasion when you'll put the level strand from option to left straightaway.

Lay the first collapsed strand under the spine, string another collapsed strand into its circle. Get the lower strands through the top circle. What's more, fix.

Continue onward and work step by step down in size.

Make sure to push the strands up to fix - get the base of the center (spine) strand with one hand and with another, push the strands up. When you're set, drag the periphery downwards to meet the base of the center strand.

At that point, give it an unpleasant trim. This helps control the shape as well as assists with brushing the strands out. The shorter the strands, the simpler, to be completely forthright. It additionally assists in having an extremely sharp pair of texture shears!

After an unpleasant trim, place the feather on a tough surface as you'll be using a creature brush to brush out the cording. The brush will harm any sensitive or wood surface, so I propose using a self-mending cutting mat or even a smoothed cardboard box.

When brushing, start at the spine and drive hard into the cording. It'll take a few hard strokes to get that lovely, delicate periphery.

Work your way down. At the point when you're at the base, hold the bottom of the spine while brushing - you don't need the brush to yank any strands off! Next, you'll need to harden the feather. The cording is delicate to such an extent that it'll merely tumble if you get it and attempt to hang it. Give it splash, or two, and permit to go after at any rate two or three hours.

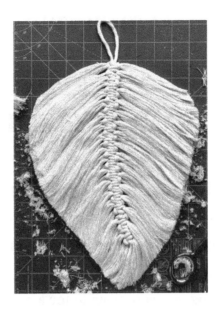

When your feather has hardened up a piece, you would now be able to return and give it the last trim. This, I would state, is the most testing part. Relax. It's smarter to trim not precisely more! Furthermore, you may need to alter your trim contingent upon how regularly you're moving the piece. When you're finished cutting, you can even give it another wanderer of texture stiffener for good measure. And afterwards, you'll be prepared to hang your piece!

CHAPTER TWO

PROJECT TWO: TASSEL AND MACRAMÉ KEY-CHAINS

Arranged bit by bit macramé guidelines. Presently you can macramé simple, lovable DIY key-rings that utilization stuff you have close by—make them as necessary or as extravagant as you'd like. These DIY macramé key-chains utilize basic knots, essential decorations, and wooden beads. The absolute best and unobtrusive blessing you can provide for a companion that they will esteem! Additionally, incredible practice for your new macramé abilities!

Why make DIY macramé key-chains? If you need a reason to create a custom key-chain, we have you:

• Update the key-chain you've had since before you can recall

• Create a charming key-ring for the pet-sitter

• Give a lot of keys to a believed neighbor so when you lock yourself out, you don't need to break into your place

• Decorate your knapsack

- Decorate your handbag

- Create the snazziest gear tag on the baggage merry go round

- Get sorted out by making a different key-ring for every one of those little rewards cards

- Stocking stuffers, birthday presents, present wrap additional items

Materials Needed

- 1" key rings

- 3/16" standard cotton channeling string

- Beads

- Embroidery floss or yarn

- Small elastic band (key-chain #4 as it were)

- Scissors

#1: Square knot with a bead.

#2: Striped clove hitch.

#3: Beads with short decoration.

#4: Folded twist.

#5: Beads with a long tuft.

#6: Half knots.

Instructions to Make Key-chains With Square Knots

How about we start with key-chains #1 and #6. They're made with a straightforward square knot—and it's incomplete, however extravagant sister, the half square knot.

- For both, you'll start with two 50″ or so bits of string. Circle each through the key-ring with a larkspur knot, making the outside strands around 2/3 the length of the rope.

- For key-chain #1, make around five square knots, including the bead, make a half square knot beneath it, and tie the rest off in a decoration.

- For key-chain #6, make around 16 half square knots and finish it with decoration.

- To give your decoration the ideal extravagant neck, utilize your preferred shades of weaving string.

- Separate the line at the closures, trim it up, and you're done!

Tip: To cut the base of the decoration entirely straight, press it level and wrap it with a bit of tape. Cut the tape down the middle,

evacuate it, and wonder about the ideal periphery.

Instructions to Make Key-chains With Beads and Tassels

Key-chains #3 and #5, utilize a similar method, however, differ up the number of beads and length of the tuft.

• For both, you'll start by tying a 10-16" bit of yarn to your key-ring with a larkspur knot.

• Add the globules.

• Cut yarn for decoration—we utilized around 20 bits of wool. (You pick the length and cushiness. Make it twice the length you need your decoration.) Center it under the globule and tie it on with a basic knot. Straighten out your beads and decoration and twofold the knot.

• Fold the tuft down the middle and wrap the neck with yarn or weaving floss.

• Trim the closures. That is it!

Step by Step Instructions to Make A Striped Clove Hitch Key-chain

Key-chain #2 may look extravagant and entangled—yet it just takes two essential knots to get its sharp custom shading palette.

• Start with two 20″ or so bits of rope (you can generally cut them shorter, so it's smarter to begin long). Circle each through the key-ring with a larkspur knot, making the outside strands about somewhat longer than ones within.

- Add vertical clove hitch fastens with a couple of various shades of yarn.

- Make a full square knot in the center.

- Add another arrangement of vertical clove hitches, turning around what you did on the top.

- A quick trim of the closures polishes it off.

Step by Step Instructions to Make A Folded Braid Key-chain

Key-chain #4 is straightforward.

- Cut three bits of rope somewhat more than twice the length you need the completed custom key-chain.

- Stack them, even the strands, and wrap one end with a little elastic band a couple of crawls from the closures.

- Do a straightforward twist. Stop when you're same good ways from the finishes from the elastic band is.

- Loop one end through the key-chain. If you'd like, but the elastic band around the two closures to hold them set up.

- Start the neck directly under the mesh. You can cut the elastic band free as you begin to wrap the neck with weaving floss.

- Tie knots in the closures of the line to wrap it up.

CHAPTER THREE

PROJECT THREE: MACRAMÉ GARLAND WITH WOOD BEADS

An exquisite wreath produced using cautiously knotting macramé harmony. Adhere to the guidelines bit by bit, and you can make it as well!

Materials Needed:

- Macramé yarn

- Sharp scissors (I like using haircutting scissors)

- Wood globules (I utilized some somewhat bigger ones I had, I lied rotating marginally various sizes)

- Hairbrush (if you need to brush out the edges once more)

For my laurel, I utilized 23 wooden beads strung on a 10 foot bit of macramé string. I needed it to be extended, so I might tell it's

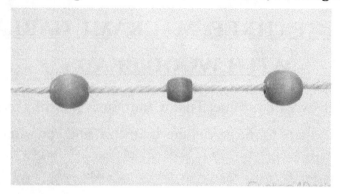

on a Christmas tree sooner rather than later.

For my length of laurel, you have to knot 22 little bits of macramé inside and out.

Furthermore, when you make one bit of macramé in the middle of the above wood globules, you have to cut 6 bits of 40-inch macramé yarn, which you at that point need to repeat multiple times or anyway long you need your laurel. I needed to cut 132 bits of 40-inch macramé yarn strings.

Does that bode well? So I explicitly utilized:

•   10 foot bit of yarn (for wreath base)

•   23 wooden globules

- 132 bits of 40-inch macramé yarn

I began my learner macramé festoon by collapsing the 40-inch bits of macramé down the middle and circling them onto the base string with Lark's Head knots as demonstrated as follows.

Try to pull them tight and repeat multiple times.

After that, you need to make square knots. Make sure to interchange that string, which is put on top.

After making a column, you need to counterbalance the knots so you can make a pyramid toward the end.

Then, the time has come to make a corner to corner Half Hitch knots on each side of the little macramé triangle/pyramid.

These sorts of knots are fundamentally circles set on to the external string on each side that, at that point, meet at the focal point of the piece.

And afterwards, the laurel is nearly done. You can either decided to leave the festoon open, or you can tie each macramé off into a little tuft at the base, which I will show you beneath.

CHAPTER FOUR

PROJECT FOUR: MACRAMÉ JAR HANGER

These look so pretty – I'm fixating on them. It will cost you a couple of jars or yoghurt and some macramé line. Simple, reasonable, and beautiful. Macramé is a unique little something that looks truly confused until you plunk down and attempt it, and afterwards you understand it's not so much that hard. It just takes a touch of fixation.

Materials Needed

• Scissors

• Jars

• Macramé Cording – I utilized the macramé cording, and it worked incredibly.

• Fairy lights to stuff in the jars when you are finished. I utilized battery worked pixie lights. (Discover placing a genuine sparkle in there to be somewhat alarming so be cautious).

Macramé Cording – comes in all extraordinary rope sizes and hues

Macramé Kit! It accompanies the cording and rings all set!

Macramé Wood Rings – love the beautiful way hearty these are

I isolated this out into gradual steps; however, don't let that overpower you. Trust me, and when you get moving, it doesn't take long!

One thing to note, which may be clear, yet I'm referencing it in any case: I washed my yoghurt jars and took the stickers off. I plan on using a touch of goo gone to get all the sticker buildup off; however, my goo went is presently stored.

Stage 1: Measure out your cording. You can make this as long or short as you need. Here's the specific equation I utilized.

Length of hanger x 2 + length of jar + 10 inches. I picked 18 crawls for my hanger length, so I allotted that with the string twice, at that point included the stature of my jar, included another 10 inches, and cut my string there. I saw this length as MORE than enough!

Stage 2: Now that you have your first bit of cording cut, you need to cut three additional pieces precisely the same length for a sum of four equivalent bits of cording.

Stage 3: Fold the lines fifty-fifty. Tie a knot at the head of the crease. This will be the charming little hanger part. Tidy up the knot by pulling on the ropes, so it's quite slick.

Stage 4: Now hang it up on something – a bureau handle, a door handle, and so on. I thought that it was a lot simpler to tie the knots when it was hanging (even though for this instructional exercise, I spread it out, so it was more straightforward for you to see.)

Stage 5: Take any two lines and tie a knot a little way down. Do this with everyone until you have something like this? Make the knots even right around.

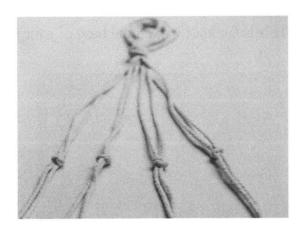

Stage 6: Now. Take two of the knots you simply made and snatch one line from every last one of those knots and tie those strings along with another knot.

Go right around until you have four knots. Ensure they are, for the most part, equivalent. This will be your second column of knots, and you will see the hanger begin shaping. This is your light second!

Stage 7: Repeat stage 6 and make another, third column of knots. With these little jars, I saw three lines of knots as the best.

Stage 8: Put your little jar in there and ensure it fits. If it doesn't, at that point, simply change your knots a piece or stretch them out as much as could be expected under the circumstances.

If it fits in there – simply tie all the last details at the base into a primary knot. This huge knot will be the base of your jar hanger.

Stage 9: You can trim the overabundance hanging from the knot or keep it long. Stuff each jar with the pixie lights. Presently hang them up and appreciate.

You're finished!

CHAPTER FIVE

PROJECT FIVE: MACRAMÉ WALL HANGING

Macramé is fantastic, so now's an ideal opportunity to break out your knot-tying aptitudes. With all the showcases at various Outfitters and macramé curtains illuminating all over the place, you can make your version of this wall craft pattern. As opposed to making a customary macramé project with rope, we utilized an elective material: pullover texture! It worked mystically. The final product was a lovely wall hanging that would be immaculate to hang in your home, use as a setting at a gathering, or even as chic DIY wedding stylistic layout. Also, you just need two materials to make it! You've most likely observed that goliath last macramé wall hangings. Indeed, everybody needs to begin someplace! So here is a basic yet polished form for any amateur!

Materials

– Wooden dowel

– Jersey texture

Instruments:

– Fabric scissors

Directions:

1. Cut slender pieces of texture around 1 inch by 10 feet. (Knotting the composition makes the last project a lot shorter. Our 10-foot strips made a 3 ½ foot wall hanging).

2. Overlap a texture strip into equal parts and slide the circle end under the dowel. String the open closures of the texture through the circle and pull it tight to make sure about over the dowel. Repeat with each segment of texture, putting them around 1 inch separated until you arrive at the finish of the dowel.

3. Make a line of fundamental knots, fixing them as near the dowel as you need (We left about an inch between our knot and dowel).

4. Make a column of square knots a couple of crawls beneath your underlying line of essential knots (read underneath for bit by bit square knot directions!). At that point directly underneath, include a second line of square knots using a similar texture strip, making a twofold square knot design.

5. Move a couple of crawls underneath, and include another column of square knots beginning two strips in from the edge. At

that point directly underneath, add a third column of square knots using a similar texture strip, making the same twofold square knot design.

6. Move a couple of crawls beneath, and make another column of square knots using the texture takes from the mainline. At that point directly underneath, include a fourth line of square knots using a similar texture strip, making the same twofold square knot design.

7. Get it ;)? Make extra lines of knots (either twofold square or fundamental knots) until your design is finished.

8. Cut the finishes of the texture strips with the goal that they are even. Your most brief strip will decide the length of your wall hanging.

First of all, you have to cut some long pieces of texture. By longing, we don't mean a yard, and we mean three, four, or perhaps five yards. Hold up! Each piece will be collapsed into equal parts and afterwards knotted so that the length will diminish considerably.

Crease a texture strip fifty-fifty and afterwards wrap the circle end around your dowel. Pull the open closures of the texture strip through the circle and fix it to tie down it to the dowel. Repeat this progression with different strips. This part is somewhat similar to throwing on for every one of you knitters out there. Even though it's not time to sew, it's an ideal opportunity to knot. How about we get to it!

We're going, beginning with, an essential knot. You've done this previously, perhaps even today, when you tied your shoes. Make one column of fundamental knots by collapsing one strip over the other and getting it through. Fix your knot as near the dowel as

you need. We left about an inch in between our knot and dowel. Sufficiently simple, eh? Curve! Here's a progressively convoluted knot for you: the square knot.

The square knot is a typical macramé knot, and it's very basic once you get its hang. You'll have to utilize four pieces of texture. We should all beginning on a similar side to make the directions simpler, alright? So move to the extreme right half of your project. Take the four texture strips on the extreme right and separate them from the rest. Using the strip on the extreme left (that is the fourth strip in from the correct side of your project) lay it over the center two making a "four." It ought to be opposite to the center two pieces. Weave it under the texture strip on the extreme right. At that point, take the strip on the extreme right and acquire it under the two the center and through the circle on the left. Pull this tight-ish (we left our own a small piece free as should be obvious). Presently make a similar knot again to finish your square. Ta-dah! We bent over our square knots and made a full column of them.

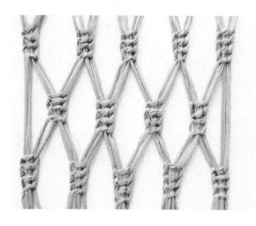

We included a second line of double square knots beginning two strips in from the edge to make all the more an example (jewels!). At that point, we included a third column of twofold square knots using a similar texture strips as the mainline, and to complete, we tied a line of essential knots falling corner to corner.

At the point when you complete the process of knotting, trim the finishes with the goal that you have a decent spotless line at the base of your wall hanging.

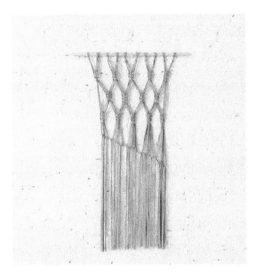

Go forward and make yourself another wall hanging!

CHAPTER SIX

PROJECT SIX: MACRAMÉ NECKLACE

Macramé has gotten fiercely well-known over the most recent few years for its extraordinary normal and high quality tasteful. Making macramé yourself gives such a significant amount of opportunity to create unique pieces. Here is an essential DIY macramé necklace, ideal for blending with the entirety of your mid-year outfits! These macramé necklaces are so lovely and will make delightful blessings and a particularly sweet adornment for an evening to remember!

Making Your Necklace

Our DIY macramé necklace utilizes a progression of the essential macramé knots — the square knot. To make this necklace, you will require a chain and adornment discoveries. We discovered our copper chain at our nearby adornments store and afterward utilized a lobster fasten with two bounce rings. We used a copper key-ring for our inside; however, don't hesitate to pick another sort of metal that better accommodates your style! While you are at your gems store, you can likewise select little globules to include in your macramé weaving. Simply ensure that the beads are a similar thickness as your string or the beads will sneak off! The white material is cotton twine, and the greyish material is hemp rope. When you have your materials prepared, follow the bit by bit photographs instructional exercise beneath to plait your DIY macramé necklace.

Stage 1: What You Need:

1.   Hemp or hemp-like string

2.   Beads

3.   Scissors

•   Measure to what extent you need the necklace to be, by holding it around your neck at the favored length. Include some additional length so you have enough to close it with.

•   The string that goes "outwardly" of the necklace will be genuinely long, roughly 7, 5 – 8 meters.

Stage 2: How to Do the Knots:

1.   Start by making an ordinary knot with a little circle on top.

2.   Start on the right side by releasing the longest string over the two shorter strings in the center.

3.   Take the string to one side over the string that you put over the strings in the center.

4.   Take a similar string (the left string) under the briefest strings.

5.   Continue with the same string by getting it through the opening made by the correct string.

6. Tighten by pulling the two most extended strings to frame a knot. There will be a bit "bump" on the left side.

7. Then you make a similar advance over once more. It is essential to begin the knot from the same side each an ideal opportunity to get it swirly.

8. Repeat this the same number of times you feel like it before you put on a bead. It is a smart thought to gauge the length if you need the beads to be a similar length separated from one another.

Stage 3: Putting on a Bead:

1.   Thread the globule on to the two briefest strings and bring
        it up to where you have interlaced.

2.   Do a similar knot as in the past; simply make sure to do it
under the globule.

3.   Tighten and keep interlacing till the following point where
you need to put another bead.

Stage 4: Finishing It:

1. To completion the necklace, you take the two briefest strings and put them through the circle and inside the knot. Keep plaiting till the end string is made sure about.

2. To fix the two most extended strings, you can do a typical knot on every one of the sides. Attempt to get it as near the necklace as could be expected under the circumstances, to make it look as decent as could reasonably be expected.

3. Cut of free strings, however, not very near the knots as they can relax.

Stage 5: Finished Product:

1.   The necklace should then look something like this.

CHAPTER SEVEN

PROJECT SEVEN: MACRAMÉ PLANT HANGER

This straightforward macramé plant hanger DIY is ideal for spring. It is a simple and economical project costing under $3. Prepare a few macramé plant holders to put close to each window in your home. A basic macramé plant hanger that you can make out of unbiased twine or go for something splendid and bright! Since I was making up a couple of additional for my pantry re-try and association post I have been promising, I figured it would be an ideal opportunity to return to the subject. We have been striving to wrap up our pantry makeover by painting the cupboards, making association, and sewing crate liners.

In any room, I love to add regular surfaces and greenery to liven up space and give it a comfortable vibe. There is something in particular about adding live plants to rooms that lights up and revives rooms. These macramé plant hangers do only that. When you get its hang, you will be whipping out these children left and right. They make incredible blessings! The remarkable thing about these plant hangers, other than that they take no time and cash, is that you can modify the length to suit any estimate plant.

What is the best string for macramé?

You have a few unique options for this plant hanger, and I picked jute since it is anything but difficult to work with, and I love the shading and surface. You could likewise utilize a dainty macramé string from a craft store or even nylon clothesline.

Is macramé simple?

Indeed it very well maybe. Macramé can be as straightforward or as entangled as you make it. If you are new to macramé, start with simple projects like this one, or this wall hanging. When you get its hang, then you can attempt increasingly confounded ones with progressively troublesome knots and various surfaces.

To what extent does it take to make a macramé plant holder?

This is a fundamental macramé project that will take you around short ways all the way to make.

Supplies you should do this project:

- Jute

- Scissors

- Something to hang your plant hanger-on. I utilized a nail to do the project and afterward draped them from the roof using snares.

- Plants in little pots. I utilized small pots from IKEA. However, most other small pots would work.

Step by step instructions to Make A Macramé Plant Hanger

Stage 1: Cut the Cord

1. Start by removing nine bits of jute twine to your ideal length. If you needn't bother with the hanger to be extra-long and to suit a typical size plant, start with 100" pieces.

2. Fold the strings fifty-fifty, and tie a little string in the center. At the point when you hold the strings by that small string, you should wind up with 18 pieces that are a large portion of the length you initially began with.

3. Hang the project from a nail in the wall so that you can work with it all the more without any problem. (You could do this by snapping a photo down, and working with the nail that was hanging it.) You can likewise work this

project on a table. It is only a little more straightforward when it is hanging.

Stage 2: Create Macramé Braids and Knots

1. Divide the 18 strings into three areas with six lines each.

2. Braid each area until you arrive at the ideal length. For an extra-long plant hanger, this will be around 24″. For only an average period, interlace about 14″.

3. Tie a knot toward the finish of each mesh.

4. Next, go down from the mesh knot about 6″ (or less if you are making a minuscule one). Separation the base of the plait into equal parts, with the goal that you have three pieces on each side. Go along with one twist to the following one over by tying three from each twist (six aggregate) with a knot. Repeat in a rounbeadout manner until each of the three meshes are associated.

5. Go down about another 6″ (or less if you are making a little one) and make another line of knots.

Stage 3: Finish Macramé Plant Hanger with Large Knot

1. Finally, go down a last 6″ and make one monster knot with every one of the 18 pieces.

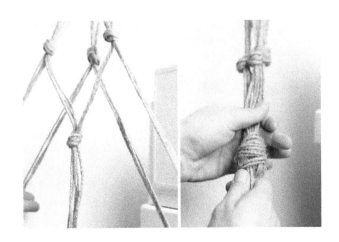

2. Trim the strings.

3.　　Place pruned plants into the macramé plant holder. That is it.

Well... It made me think how lovely these plant hangers would be with minuscule succulents. Simply make the interlace lengths, and spaces between the knots, littler to take into consideration such a short course of action.

CHAPTER EIGHT

PROJECT EIGHT: MINI MACRAMÉ CHRISTMAS ORNAMENTS

I intended to make these macramé Christmas ornaments a year ago and used up all available time to consummate them, so they were on the exceptionally head of my rundown this year. I attempted some with yarn a year ago; however, it was excessively slight, and they were too difficult to even think about making. This year I found the reasonable ideal rope at the dollar store, and love the fantastic way these turned out. They were economical to make, and moderately simple once you get its hang. I am one of those individuals who can't sew or stitch, so if you are in almost the same situation, there's a promise for you as well. Enrich your Christmas tree with a boho vibe by rehearsing your macramé abilities on smaller than usual macramé ornaments! Flawless Christmas presents for companions as well!

Materials for Christmas Macramé Ornaments

- Macramé string or rope

- Twigs

- Hairbrush or brush

- Masking tape

- Scissors

Getting the Cords On To the Twig

To begin, cut a little twig and utilize the songbird's head knot to connect six lines to the top. I used rope, so before I added it to the

twig, I un-wound it and diverted it from 3 handles to single employ. Each string ought to be around 2 feet in length.

To tie a warbler's head knot, first, overlay the string into equal parts and afterwards lie the center of it over the head of the twig.

Crease the circle over the rear of the twig, and afterwards get the two finishes through the top. Pull tight. Repeat for each of the six strings.

Square Knot Mini Macramé Christmas Ornament

First Square Knot

When the ropes are onto the twig, it's an ideal opportunity to begin the mainline, which will be three square knots. These knots are attached with four strings, so start on the forgetful part about it and separate the first four ropes.

To make the square knot take the left-hand rope to haul it out so it would appear that a number "4" shape is framing.

Next, fold the finish of the first string under the fourth string.

At that point, bring the finish of the fourth string up and behind the center two ropes and through the space between the first and second line that resembles the four.

Pull the closures of the first and fourth rope to fix and move that knot up to the top. This is the first half of a square knot.

For the other 50% of the square knot, you will do precisely the same thing; however, in the other course. You're going to make your "4" shape with the first and fourth rope, however, with the "4" in reverse, confronting the right side.

At that point, pull the first rope over the fourth.

At that point, feed the tail of the first rope under the second and third-string and up through the opening of the "4" shape.

Pull the closures of the first and fourth string to fix, and you have your first square knot.

Continue working in segments of four ropes. Bind another square knot and another square knot to make three along the top line.

For the subsequent column, you're just going to do 2 square knots. To do this, beginning by isolating out the first to ropes. The following four strings are for the subsequent square knot on line 2, trailed by the following one. That will leave the other two strings out on the opposite end as well.

For the third line, utilize just the inside four ropes of the line to tie one square knot.

You will discover you may need to change your strain, attempt to keep the knots all similarly fixed and separated.

For line 4, repeat column 2 with 2 square knots once more, forgetting about the two lines on either side.

For line 5, repeat column 1 with 3 square knots.

Line 6 - Half Hitch Knot

You could complete this ornament there with the square knots, or as I added, a column of half hitch knots.

To do the half hitch knot, take the first string in the column, and pull over the piece on a flat plane. This will be your lead line.

Take the second string from behind and over the lead and through the opening you've made. Presently do that definite knot again with the equivalent second line. That is a one-half hitch.

Continue along with the remainder of the strings, taking consideration to keep the first chain pulled across evenly and straight bowing different lines around it.

To fix the knots, pull the lead line.

Completing the Ornament

To complete the piece, cut the closures straight over, or into a descending or upwards "V" at the base.

At that point, utilize a hairbrush or brush to brush out the line and make the periphery base. You may need to re-trim the shape a brief time after you brush it out.

At long last trim, the finishes of the twig, and add a bit of rope to hang the ornament from.

Slanting Half Hitch Mini Macramé Ornament

Start this ornament by adding six lines to a twig with a songbird's knot, much the same as the first.

To make this ornament, you make three lines of the corner to corner half hitch knots that structure a "V."

The primary string will be your lead rope, holding it at a corner to corner this time rather than evenly, circle the second line up and over it, and through the gap you've made. At that point, do that again with the second string to finish the half hitch knot.

Holding the lead rope immovably at an inclining, attach a half hitch with the third rope marginally let down, on the slanting of your lead string.

Repeat this for the first six ropes.

At that point, get the last line, the twelfth string on the extreme right, and use it as the lead rope and bind half hitches from the other heading to meet in the middle.

Line 2-3

For line 2, repeat equivalent to push 1. However, this time when you get together on the inside, you can utilize the string from the opposite side to interface the two sides of the "V" together, as found in picture 2 of the collection above.

To complete the ornament, trim the edges of the rope along the base, and brush out the periphery simply like the first.

At long last trim, the twig finishes and includes a hanging string.

CHAPTER NINE

PROJECT NINE: MACRAMÉ BAG

Irrespective of what you do, the more you practice, the better you get, and I need to state we've been truly getting a charge out of letting loose a little creation macramé rope bags, enjoyable to make and (fortunately) goodness so on the pattern at present! You may have seen our other variant, and this new one expands on that style that we did and includes a couple of additional means as well. Lessen your waste while brandishing your new high-quality macramé bag at the market! Ideal for looking for produce! Appreciate knotting!

What You'll Need

- String

- Scissors

- 2 gold bounce ring

- Needle and string

For this one, we have done a macramé strap just as a macramé knotted bag area. All things considered, if you needed to do the knotted bag segment simply, you could simply join a calfskin strap to the gold rings. It's absolutely up to you!

To Make the Handle

This strap may glance overwhelming, yet truly it's extremely only one underhand knot style done a couple of various ways. Peruse on and see!

We'll start by knotting the strap of the bag. You'll have to knot every 50% of the strap independently, so the length of each bit of string should be on behalf of the all-out length of the strap, times

4. The straps were to be a sum of 46cm (18"), so the string pieces we cut were half of that occasion 4.

Crease the string into equal parts and knot it on your band using the collapsed end.

Complete four knots.

Beginning with the knot on the right, take the inward string and circle it around the external string.

Fix the knot, and this is what it ought to resemble.

Repeat the last knot, just using the following string this time.

This is a side of the knots that were done.

Knot the opposite side of the straps using the equivalent knotting strategy, just switching the heading this time.

This are the two sides done.

Repeat this for the two sides multiple times.

Once more, using the equivalent knotting strategy, interface the two strands by expanding the knots.

This is what the expanding line resembles.

Repeat these all-inclusive lines multiple times.

At that point, alter the course and knot from left to directly for the following three lines.

At that point, repeat the side knots. When you've done this, you have completed a large portion of the strap!

Repeat this for the other strap and circle, and we'll associate them later on.

To polish off the knot-work, repeat a similar knot.

Cut off one of the strands in the knot; at that point, proceed with the tying another knot using the following strand.

This is what the completed end will resemble.

To connect the straps, line up the closures and sew along with needle and string.

Making the Main Part of The Bag

To make the body of the rope bag, cut 10 bits of string that are multiple times the ideal length of your bag. The bag we made is

15" (39cm). Knot it onto the gold band using the collapsed end like previously.

The whole body of the rope bag will be finished with box knots. Taking two strings as an afterthought, circle it around the two center strands.

Repeat the knot and pull the knot tight.

Repeat the knots on the remainder of the strands, make sure to keep the separations between the knots and the loops the

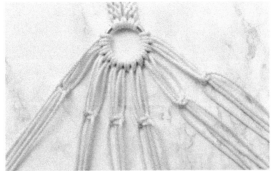

equivalent. We did our own 3" down from the band.

Keep doing box knots for the subsequent line, just using the strings one strand over this time.

Knot 3 columns of box knots on the two sides, before knotting the

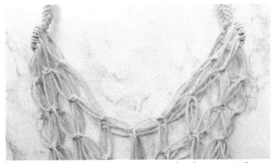

hands of the bag by using two strands from either side.

Keep doing box knots until the bag is the size you are after. Clip off the closures of the strings if you don't need any tuft finishes,

and spot a touch of paste into the knots to make sure about them. Flip the bag out.

CHAPTER TEN

PROJECT TEN: MINI PUMPKIN MACRAMÉ HANGER

Prepare for the Halloween season and hotshot your pumpkins in another manner! Macramé pumpkin hangers!

Supplies Needed

• Black yarn or string

• Metal ring

• Wooden beads

• Scissors

Methodology

Cut five strands of yarn that are about 3-times the length that you need the completed hanger to be. Overlap the strands fifty-fifty and circle through the metal band.

Next, separate the yarn strands into gatherings of two.

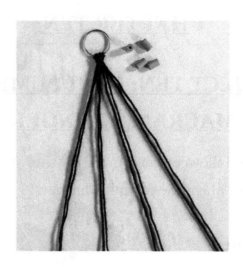

Tie each gathering into a knot. String a wooden bead onto each strand, at that point, tie another knot just beneath the bit.

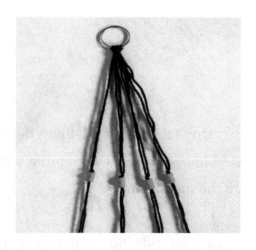

A couple of crawls down, tie another line of knots.

Next, integrate two nearby strings and repeat with each string. At that point, integrate the last string with the first. Repeat this

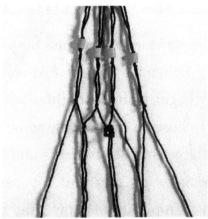

procedure and tie another line of strings together.

At last, integrate all the strings in a single enormous knot.

Spot your little pumpkins into your macramé hanger and show!

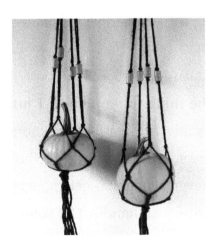

CHAPTER ELEVEN

PROJECT ELEVEN: BOHEMIAN MACRAMÉ MIRROR WALL HANGING

Searching for a simple starter macramé project? At that point, this a la mode DIY Bohemian Macramé Mirror Wall Hanging is an excellent spot to begin. Only two or three knots to learn for one unusual project. I chose to fiddle with some actual macramé! There are such a large number of knots and approaches to tie them in the specialty of macramé, it can appear to be overpowering and a simple craft to stay away from. To begin on the first genuine endeavor I chose to go with a straightforward project. I have my eye on a plant hanger type macramé reflect that I discovered someplace. I would have recently gotten it and considered it daily, and then again, actually, I previously had the materials to make it myself. This boho-chic DIY project joins style with work by making a cool method to balance a mirror on the wall!

The not get make the thing too muddled. I just thought knots, square knots, and some ordinary basic knots in this project carefully. The square knots are the hardest to hold your head over from the start. However, when you get the hang of tying them, they become a lot simpler to handle. Get some macramé string, and how about we begin!

Supplies:

- Macramé Cording: 4mm

- Octagon Mirror

- Wood Ring: 2 inch

- Wood Beads: 25mm w/10mm Hole Size

- Sharp Scissors

Guidelines:

Cut 4 bits of macramé cording into 108 inches (or 3yds) areas.

Overlap the strips into equal parts and tie each of the four on the wood circle using a Lark's Head knot. Pull the knots tight and

near one another. Separate two out of the Lark's Head knots and begin integrating them with a square knot.

Tie two square knots.

Begin integrating two square knots with the subsequent two Lark's Head knots.

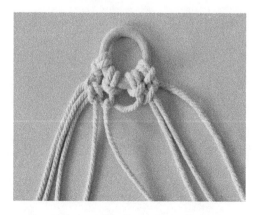

As you start the subsequent square knot, circle it through one of the sides of the other two square knots to consolidate them into one substantial full square knot.

Tie 7 square knots going down the two sides and inside and out.

Split off the closures subsequent to tying the knots—three strings for each side and 4 in the inside. Add tape to the closures of the cording to seal the frayed finishes. This will make it simpler to include the beads. Well done! That was the crucial step! The rest is merely tying simple knots and getting the sides even.

Add one bead to every one of the two side cording lines. Tie a knot under the globule on the two sides, making them even. Tie the four lines in the middle into a plain or (Overhand knot) around 1/14 inch beneath the beads.

Take one string from the middle and add it to the two lines on the sides. Then, tie the three together in a knot on the two sides. Include one of the three side cording to the rear of the mirror to

hold it consistent. Add the mirror to get the knot lengths even.

Tie straightforward knots in every one of the three side ropes at the base left and right of the mirror. Separate the three sides' lines once more. Send one on each side to the rear of the mirror and welcome two on each side on the facade of the mirror and tie them into a knot.

Turn the mirror over and tie the entirety of the strings together. Turn the mirror back finished and disengage the front knot. Slip the back ropes inside the knot and retighten the knot. Chop the cording closes down to around 14 inches. Pull the finishes or the cording free and let them brawl. Brush the finishes of the cording with a brush to cushion closes. Hang and appreciate it!

CHAPTER TWELVE

PROJECT TWELVE: MACRAMÉ FRIENDSHIP BRACELET WATCH

This Friendship Bracelet Watch pursues the interlacing pattern with zeal and style! Give a beautiful and fun blessing to your best friend by making coordinating closest companion watches with sewed groups!

For this project, you will require:

- A watch face with posts

- Craft floss or weaving floss

- Crimp closes (discretionary) – mine is 20mm

- Jump rings and conclusion (discretionary)

To begin, you'll require your watch face and your floss. I'm using craft floss in orange, white, and a minty blue kind of shading. Cut strips that are around 48 inches in length. For this watch face,

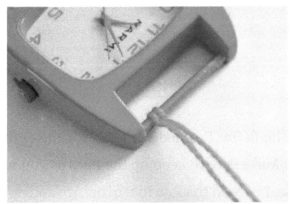

you'll require 10 of these long strands for each side (however, just cut ten at present, leave the others until you're prepared to begin the opposite side).

We're going to lash each bit of floss onto the bar to start making our strap. Put the finishes of one great bit of floss together and snatch the end. Push it through the bar and afterward get the finishes through the circle you made merely like in the pics above.

Pull tight to hook on. Proceed with this for the entirety of your cuts of floss. Make sure to keep up the hues as you need them in your example. I needed thick stripes of orange and mint and more

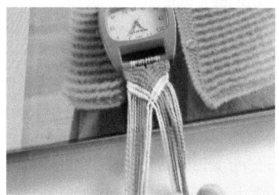

slender pieces of white. Accordingly, my request went: orange, orange, white, mint, mint, mint, mint, white, orange, and orange.

Furthermore, presently you simply start your companionship interlacing. Since we hooked onto the post, we're not going to have that abnormal clustered up thing that occurs on most fellowship bracelets that begin with a knot. Quite cool, huh?

You have the choice of twisting the closures like some other companionship armband and afterwards tying shut when you wear it. This isn't the prettiest choice; however, it will work truly well. In any case, if you need to utilize terminations, continue perusing.

At the point when you get the length, you need to take a good measure of paste and run a line where you'll have to cut. Rub the dough into the strings on both the front and posteriors. This will keep the mesh immovably together for our subsequent stage. I utilized Aleene's brisk dry shabby paste since I'm appallingly eager.

One thing to note is that fellowship twists have a not too bad measure of giving in them. I didn't think about this, and after a couple of years, I've needed to abbreviate my straps. You might need to feel free to make the watch a weensy piece tight. It might be awkward that first wear, yet it will be ideal a couple of hours in.

Utilize sharp scissors to slice through your strap in the region you applied the paste. Perceive how well it stays together? Feel free to

run a piece on the conclusion to help forestall fraying.

Spot your brace onto the finish of the straps and use pincers to clip firmly on. Finish the finishes with a bounce ring on one and a hop ring and conclusion on the other.

CHAPTER THIRTEEN

PROJECT THIRTEEN: MACRAMÉ CURTAIN

When one is starting to make the real drape, I made 14 gatherings of rope, each collection with four strands that were every one of the 100 inches in length. I thought that it was made a neater knot at the head of the window ornament to cut two strands of rope that were double the required length (so 200 inches), and afterward I draped the strands over the pole at the center point and attached a knot to make a four-strand gathering. Since doing this procedure with large ropes is a lot greater scale than the yarn, you'll need to discover something to hang your bar from so you let your rope hang underneath it. I used to be enamored with those fun beaded curtains that isolated rooms, however, to be completely forthright, the globules were a touch of irritating... Here's a cutting edge knit form that grown-ups will love too!

You can see that it's a similar standard of making the fundamental knots in the means with the yarn, however, just on a lot greater scale. I simply made the essential knot close to the head of all the 14 gatherings and afterwards made another column of knots underneath and between those knots (like in the yarn guidelines). At that point, I descended another line and made knots underneath the first knots and simply continued substituting the lines of knots until I had done the same number of columns varying. Make a point to continue venturing back as you make your knots to guarantee that you are integrating your knots with even lines. I kept a ruler convenient, so I could quantify the separation between each knot in succession and the wooden shade bar to ensure they would turn out even. When I completed five columns of even knots, I let the remainder of the strands hang down to finish the window ornament.

When you wrap up, the ropes drape your new drapery in your ideal spot. To complete, wrap covering tape (or other white tapes, I utilized "quarters tape") around the closures right where the rope hits the floor (my drape is 6 1/2 feet tall). Slice through the tape, leaving 2/3 to half of the tape flawless on the rope. This will assist the finishes by keeping from fraying extra time.

Materials Needed:

• Rope

• Wooden dowel/window ornament pole

• Masking tape

• Scissors

Guidelines

1. Tie four strands together on a froth centerboard and put pins into the top knot and at the base of the two center strands to keep those setup.

2. Take the external right strand (pink) and pass it to one side over the other center two strands. Take the external left

strand (yellow) and pass it underneath the pink strand, behind the center strands, and over the pink strand on the opposite side.

3. Pull the two strands tight. Presently you simply reverse what you did in the initial step! Take the peripheral left strand (which is presently the pink) and lay it over the center two strands. Take the furthest right strand (which is presently the yellow) and pass it underneath the pink, behind the two center strands, and over the pink on the opposite side. Pull these two strands tight until they make a knot with the woven strands from the past advance. That is the hardest part! The remainder of the means simply repeats these fundamental movements.

4. Repeat stages 1-3 with four additional strands to make another knot directly close to your first knot. Bring the two furthest right strands of the main knot to make another gathering with the furthest left two strands of the subsequent knot.

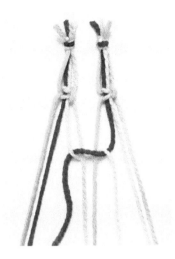

5. Repeat your fundamental knot with the newsgathering by taking the external right strand (purple) and passing it to one side over the center two strands. Take the external left strand (green) and pass it underneath the purple strand, behind the center strands, and over the purple strand on the opposite side.

6. Pull the two strands tight. Presently reverse the initial step! Take the peripheral left strand (which is presently the purple) and lay it over the center two strands. Take the furthest right strand (which is currently the green) and pass it underneath the purple, behind the two center strands, and over the purple on the opposite side. Pull these two strands tight.

7.   Divide the center gathering of strands by moving the two furthest left strands left and the two furthest right strands right. Repeat the essential knot with both the gatherings

and proceed with this procedure until you have done the same number of lines as you might want.

8.   When starting to make the real window ornament, I made 14 gatherings of rope, each gathering with four strands that were every one of the 100 inches in length. I thought that it was made a neater knot at the head of the blind to cut two strands of rope that were double the required length (so 200 inches), and afterwards I draped the strands over the bar at the center point and attached a knot to make a four-strand gathering.

9. You can see that it's a similar rule of making the essential knots in the means with the yarn, yet just on a lot greater scale. I simply made the fundamental knot close to the head of all the 14 gatherings and afterwards made another column of knots underneath and between those knots (like in the yarn guidelines). At that point, I descended another column and made knots underneath the first knots and simply continued exchanging the lines of knots until I had done the same number of lines varying. Try to continue venturing back as you make your knots to guarantee that you are integrating your knots with even columns. I kept a ruler helpful, so I could gauge the separation between each knot in succession and the wooden drapery pole to ensure they would turn out even. When I completed five columns of even knots, I let the remainder of the strands hang down to finish the window ornament.

10. Once you wrap up the ropes, balance your new window ornament in your ideal spot. To complete, wrap concealing tape (or other white tapes, I utilized "dormitory tape") around the finishes right where the rope hits the floor (my drapery is 6 1/2 feet tall). Slice through the tape, leaving 2/3 to half of the tape unblemished on the rope. This will assist the closures with keeping from fraying additional time.

CHAPTER FOURTEEN

PROJECT FOURTEEN: MACRAMÉ BOHO CHRISTMAS TREES

These delightful minimal bohemian Christmas trees will make awesome enrichment close by your Christmas tree this year! Is it accurate to say that they aren't adorable? They're too simple to do, and you can go through those piece bits of yarn or fleece. You may have to lie around. Other than the fleece you'll require:

- A scarcely any straight-ish twigs or little branches from the nursery

- Jewelry wire or other ornamental bits

- A brush or brush

- Fishing line to hang

Cut the yarn into 7-8 inch pieces. Take two strands and overlap them both down the middle to frame a circle—spot one of the circles under a twig.

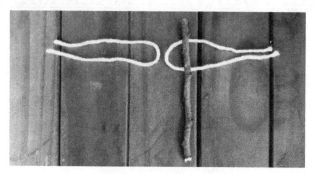

Take the circled finish of the other strand, and push the closures of the strand that is under the twig, through the circle. String the

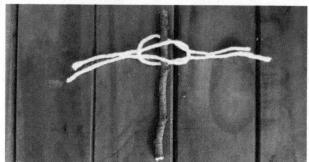

finishes of that strand through the circle that is under the twig.

Pull tight and repeat, Easy, right? If it doesn't bode well, you can watch this video to perceive how it's finished. At the point when you've included enough knotted strands, separate the strings by using a brush or a brush. The "nearly done" tree will be somewhat

floppy, so you'll have to solidify it up with some starch. We make our own using my Gran's formula. Plus, she made hers using vodka and cornstarch.

Once the boho Christmas trees are solid, trim them into a triangle shape and finish with little knick-knacks or globules. I simply made a little blossom star from adornments wire.

They take around 10 minutes so you can make an entire pack. I figure they would make dazzling presents, or you can balance them on your Christmas tree.

CHAPTER FIFTEEN

PROJECT FIFTEEN: MACRAMÉ EARRINGS

Do you ever get scared by those pretty macramé wall hangings? I do – they look so confused and tedious yet so beautiful simultaneously. Making littler variants of them takes less time and is way simpler. It's very apprentice well-disposed as well and would be incredible for individuals who like simple and quick projects. Peruse on to perceive how I made these basic and speedy to collect DIY macramé earrings that would look ideal for any spring closet! These DIY earrings are so new thus fab I simply should make them! They will look incredible, using brilliantly hued strings as well!

Supplies expected to make your DIY macramé earrings:

- Cotton Cord

- Gold Circle Jewelry Components

- Jewelry Pliers

- Earring Hooks

- Scissors

Cut 12 bits of cotton line around 12-13 creeps long. This measure

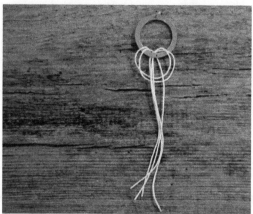

of string would be adequate for the two earrings.

Start by circling two strands of line on the hover as appeared – this is what's normally called a warbler's head knot except for we're using two strands of the line rather than one. Repeat two additional occasions and pull tight. You ought to have six strands of line on your circle.

Make a square knot on each arrangement of the line. A square knot would go through 4 strings – you should begin with the two external sets and afterwards the center arrangement of a string,

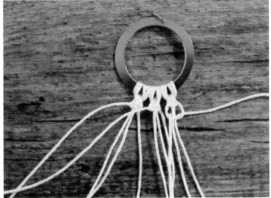

so it doesn't confound you. You should wind up with three of these square knots.

Presently we will make what's called a rotating square knot. Tally 2 from the peripheral strand, and afterwards get the four after and make your square knot. You will need to knot it somewhat farther than the upper knots to make some space. Check the following four strands and repeat a similar square knot.

For the external two strands, make a twofold half hitch knot and pull it tight, fixing up the subsequent knot with the square knot

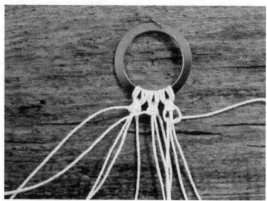

we made in sync four. Repeat on the other two strands on the opposite side.

Repeat steps 4 and 5 until you are content with the length of your macramé dangle. When you are done, remove the abundance rope. I like using water to mollify the cotton rope and manageable it, so they aren't flying all over the place. I likewise utilized a sharp device to unwind the string to make more volume as appeared on the correct stud.

At last, connect your stud snares, and your DIY macramé earrings are finished!

Wasn't excessively simple and learner inviting? These eventual an ideal evening movement with your lady friends and an ideal straightforward present for any individual who adores boho stylistic layout and embellishments. Do you love the macramé pattern?

CHAPTER SIXTEEN

PROJECT SIXTEEN: MACRAMÉ SQUARE KNOT BRACELET

It's astounding what you can make with things you have around the house when you turn on your innovative switch! Two things I love about this project are:

1) It's modest as chips: I previously had string in the cabinet, and the metal hex nuts were 3p each from the handyman store.

2) It's my sort of adornments

The wristband I made is somewhat unique to the 'twisted hex-nut armband' and uses macramé rather, which is extraordinary because I guaranteed a few instructional exercises some time back and felt somewhat awful that I hadn't composed any yet!

Square Knot

If you don't mind note: I have utilized diverse hued lines in the instructional exercise with the goal that it's simpler for you to make sense of what's going on!

1. Knot four strings together

2. Bring the left rope over the two center strings. At that point,

bring the correct rope over the left string, under the two center lines, and through the circle-shaped by the left string. Pull the privilege and left line until the knot fixes.

3. Bring the correct line over the two center ropes. At that point, bring the left rope over the correct line, under the two center lines, and through the circle framed by the correct line. Pull the

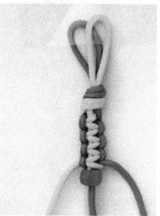

privilege and left rope until the knot fixes. Hurray... you have tied a square knot.

4. If you need to present a bead (or hex nut) at that point, just string it through onto the two center ropes at that point carry on tying square knots.

CHAPTER SEVENTEEN

PROJECT SEVENTEEN: HANGING MACRAMÉ FISHBOWL

A few projects turn out precisely how I need them to and make me grin. Different projects turn out better than I even expected and fulfill me super. And afterwards, there are those projects from time to time that turns out SO cracking cool that it makes me snicker like-a-little-school-young lady energized, and this is one of them!

I hung a fishbowl from the roof of my office in a flawless DIY macramé hanger! Indeed, you heard that right. I suspended a fishbowl from the roof and included three cute, delightfully hued pets to the family! Meet my new office aides... The motivation for this project originated from a hanging grower instructional exercise squash, A Beautiful Mess. They utilized plastic fish bowls and chain to suspend some delightful growers from the roof, and I realized I needed to have them in my office. Fishbowls... how virtuoso!

When I began arranging the subtleties of this project, my brain began to meander... "Imagine a scenario where I utilized the fish bowls for FISH rather than plants. Would you be able to drape fish from a roof? Would they be frightened they were going to dive into their demise? Or, on the other hand, would they value their a la mode burrows?" You ought to hear the discussions going on in my head now and then...

It required a significant period to make sense of the coordination of how I would securely hang the fishbowl from the roof, and at long last, I chose a simple DIY macramé hanger, which happens to be very on-pattern right now in any case. It's interesting how things from the past consistently returned style, huh? Macramé is just tying a lot of knots together, and I guarantee this project is SUPER easy to do. I've included a lot of pictures, so you know precisely where and what to knot.

Supplies:

•   50 feet nylon rope (found at the tool shop and comes in a wide range of fun hues!)

•   Glass or plastic fish bowl (I utilized a 1/2 gallon glass bowl)

•   Scissors

•   Ceiling snare

Stage 1: Cut eight bits of rope that are every 5 feet in length. Accumulate every one of the eight bits of rope and tie a huge knot toward one side, leaving 1″ – 2″ free at the top.

Stage 2: Separate the rope into four segments, with two bits of rope in each area.

Stage 3: Take one area and tie the two bits of rope into a twofold knot, leaving a 2″ hole between the principal huge knot you tied.

Stage 4: Repeat with the staying three segments of rope. Hang a fishbowl from the roof with this amazing macramé hanger!

Stage 5: Take one bit of rope from an area and join it with a bit of rope from a neighboring segment by tying a twofold knot 2″ away from the past knots you tied.

Stage 6: Repeat this procedure for the rest of the areas, using one bit of line from two unique segments.

Stage 7: Now repeat stages 5 and 6. Take one bit of rope from an area and join it with a bit of rope from a neighboring segment by tying a twofold knot 2″ away from the past knots you tied. Repeat the procedure for the rest of the segments.

Stage 8: Place your fishbowl on the head of the knotted lines, fixated on the first huge knot you tied. Pull the remaining details of rope up around the fishbowl. The bowl ought to securely rest

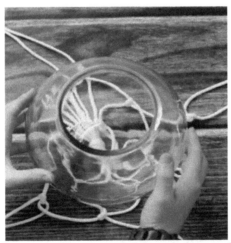

in the knotted zone. Hang a fishbowl from the roof with this wonderful macramé hanger! Give your fish a polished home and spare table space!

Stage 9: Tie a knot brushing every one of the eight pieces again about 10″ – 12″ over the head of the fishbowl. Simply ensure you leave enough space to pull the bowl in and out for cleaning. Tie another knot at the finish of the free strings and pull it as close as possible.

Stage 10: Add a roof snare where you need the fishbowl to hang. Slide the snare underneath the top knot in the middle of the eight

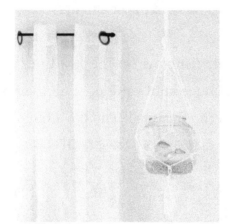

bits of rope. Ensure four bits of rope are on either side of the snare to hold the hanger set up.

Stage 11: Add your fish and appreciate!

You've heard of adding plants to a room will carry life to your space, correct? Well, these charming, little fishes do precisely the same thing, and their splendid hues simply make me grin each time I stroll by. I realized I didn't have the table space to set a fishbowl in here, yet suspending it from the roof is a major space saver, and ... it looks excessively cool, as well!

I gave the hanger and roof snare a decent pull before including the fishbowl brimming with water just to ensure I wouldn't have an all-out fiasco on my hands. I'm glad to report that it was VERY free from any danger! My young men are more seasoned now, yet I figure this would have been a magnificent arrangement when they were pretty much nothing and needed to play IN the fish tank each time I turned my back.

CHAPTER EIGHTEEN

PROJECT EIGHTEEN: MODERN DIY MACRAMÉ WALL HANGING

In case you're up for the test, here is a progressively broad project you can attempt to handle! It utilizes just 3 knots, so you ought to have the option to take care of business!

Materials Needed

- Macramé Rope – I utilized this 4mm rope – You will require (twelve) 12 – 16′ (as in feet) ropes. Recall this is a long wall hanging. That is the reason we need longer strings. You will likewise require one shorter bit of cording to fill in as your hanger. Simply tie it on there with a basic knot on either end.

- A dowel or stick – I utilized a long sewing needle. For whatever length of time that it's straight and solid and the length you need-work with what you got!

I'm so eager to give you this first macramé project. This wall hanging design was made using the accompanying fundamental macramé knots:

- Reverse Lark's Head Knot

- Square Knot and Alternating Knot

- Double Half Hitch Knot

Method for DIY Macramé Wall-hanging

Here's the bit by bit instructional exercise for this wall hanging.

1. The initial thing you need to do is knot some line around each finish of your dowel. This will fill in as the hanger for our project. It's a lot simpler to make a macramé wall hanging when it's hanging as opposed to setting down a level. You can drape this from bureau handles, door handles, a wreath hanger, or even an image hanger. Simply ensure it's durable!

2. Start by collapsing your 16′ ropes into equal parts. Ensure the finishes are even.

3. Place the circle of the rope under your dowel and string the closures of the rope through the circle. Pull tight. That is your first Reverse Lark's Head knot. (Allude to fundamental macramé knots for help).

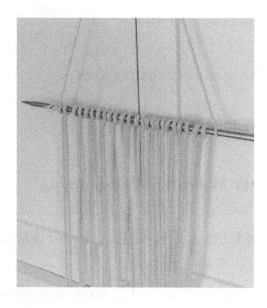

4.   Repeat Step #3 with the staying 11 lines. It should now resemble the photograph above.

5.   Make two columns of Square Knots first. (Allude to fundamental macramé knots for help).

6.   Now make two lines of Alternating Square Knots.

7.   Now make another two lines of Square knots.

8.   Continue to follow this example (2 columns of square knots, two lines of exchanging square knots) until you have a sum of 10 lines.

9. Working from left to right – make twofold half hitch knots in an askew example over your piece.

10. Now, working from option to left – make twofold half hitch knots in a corner to corner design over your piece.

11. You ought to have worked your way back over to one side!

12. Continue the example of 2 lines of Square knots then two columns of Alternating Square Knots until you have a sum of 4 lines.

13. Make two additional columns of square knots. We are going to complete the wall hanging with a lot of winding knots – which is fundamentally only a progression of half-square knots (or left side square knots). (Try not to finish the correct side of the square knot, simply make left side square knots again and again and it will winding for you.)

14. I made a sum of 13 half square knots to make this winding.

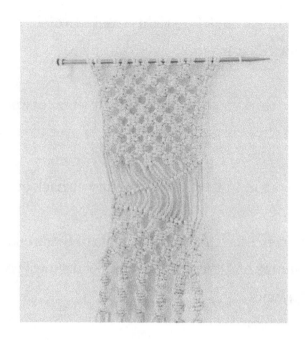

15.   Finally – I cut the base ropes into a straight line.

16.   All out measurements for my wall hanging are 6.5″ wide by 34″ long.

CHAPTER NINETEEN

PROJECT NINETEEN: MACRAMÉ CAMERA STRAP

On my last big outing, I wished the entire time I had a superior strap for my camera! While we're at home, I like using a hand strap yet for movement, and it's simply not reasonable or safe. Furthermore, as somebody who will, in general, drop things, I truly attempt to watch my valuable gear. (Once in Paris I dropped my focal point top-down a tempest channel and needed to discover a camera store to attempt to buy another one of every an abnormal English-French half and half. Not a perfect circumstance.) So! Enter this amazing DIY macramé camera strap! It's so fast to make and is ideal for spring and summer travel experiences.

Materials

Macramé string

Turn catches

Clothespins

Mechanical quality paste

Scissors

The Most Effective Method to Make A Macramé Camera Strap

Stage 1: Cut 2 lengths of macramé string, 4 yards each.

Stage 2: Fold every length of a string so that there's 1 yard on one side and 3 yards on the opposite side. Supplement the midpoints through the level piece of one turn fasten, keeping the long finishes of the strands on the exterior.

Stage 3: Pull the closures of each string through its separate circle and pull rigid around the hook.

Stage 4: Begin tying a square knot. Take the furthest left line (ought to be a long one), traverse the inside two ropes, and under the furthest right (the other long) string. At that point, bring the

correct string under the inside two and up and over the left rope. Pull this rigid. This is half of your square knot.

Stage 5: Complete the square knot by doing the reverse of stage 4. Traverse the middle two and under the left; at that point, cross the left rope under the inside two and over the right. Pull rigid, and you have finished a square knot.

Stage 6: Continue tying square knots until your camera strap is the correct length for you.

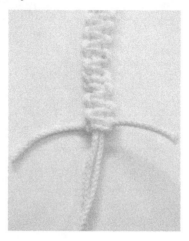

Stage 7: Trim the finishes of every one of the four ropes. Addition every one of the four lines through another turn catch. Spot a bead of paste on the finish of each string, crease the ropes over

the hook, and hold set up with clothespins while the paste dries.

When the paste is dry, evacuate the clasps and pop the strap on your camera! I love the macramé line for a camera strap since it's overly lightweight and adaptable, and comfortable around your neck. It's splendid for movement, as well — so convenient to have the option to sling your camera behind you and go. So, where are your spring ventures taking you? Trusting you get the chance to voyage away to someplace fun! Will you tote your camera on your new macramé strap!

CHAPTER TWENTY

PROJECT TWENTY: MACRAMÉ SUNSCREEN HOLDER

Upbeat about this DIY because it implies the sun is at long last out, and we need sunscreen! The previous summer, we purchased a sunscreen bottle with a carabiner that I cut to my handbag. It kept going all mid-year and was practically the best innovation ever. I always remembered sunscreen again, and we could re-apply in a hurry without delving around in my tote. This late spring, I lost the helpful travel sunscreen, so I needed to reproduce it. Since I love macramé so much, I made this charming and modest DIY macramé sunscreen holder, yet you can utilize it to convey hand sanitizer or cream as well.

Materials

+ String

+ Carabiner

+ Sunscreen

+ Small void jug

+ Tape

+ Scissors

+ Candle

Directions

1. Cut 5 bits of string about 20″ long.

2. Overlap fifty-fifty and tie one major weave in the center. Tape the knot down to keep it set up.

3. Gathering the string into five sets and knot each pair about 1″ down. Presently another 1″ down, take one string and knot it with the string from the pair close to it.

4. Proceed with this for around four columns of knots or to cover the length of your jug. Slide your jug in to check the fit and number of knots required. I put the jug on top side down for simple use.

5. When the fit is correct, attach a major knot with all the strands to hold the jug set up.

6. Over a flame, place each bit of string over the warmth to liquefy the closures and forestall fraying.

7. To polish off, join a carabiner (or key-ring) to the top knot and connect to your handbag.

The movement size jug was sufficient for all of our summer a year ago, yet you can top off varying. Presently when you need a little sunscreen clean up, you won't need to burrow around your tote. Cheerful summer!

CHAPTER TWENTY-ONE

PROJECT TWENTY-ONE: MACRAMÉ DIP-DYED MOBILE

Macramé can be as essential as only a couple of basic knots to hold your indoor house plants, a happy improvement, a fishbowl, or whatever else you can think of! Or on the other hand, it very well may be more convoluted and turn into another bit of fine art on your wall. When you get the hang of this new ability, you will knot up whatever your heart wants and adding macramé to the entirety of your stuff! Macramé is amusing to do and can be an incredible method to invest energy with companions as you tattle, drink tea, and macramé yourselves kinship bracelets!

Materials

10-in. weaving band

White twine

Scissors

Huge bowl

Texture paint

Water

Craft stick

Versatile band

Garbage bag

1. Expel the external section from the weaving band. Cut 90 bits of twine in differing lengths (no shorter than 12 in.). Overlap each

piece down the middle. Bring each collapsed piece under, finished, at that point, get the closures through the circle to make sure about.

2. Accumulate hanging twine in lots of 4 strands. Knot together to make sure about a large portion of an inch beneath the weaving circle. Repeat right around the circle.

3. Get 2 bits of twine from the main bundle and knot with 2 bits of twine from the second pack a large portion of an inch

underneath the principal column of knots. Repeat right around the circle.

4. In a huge bowl, utilize a craft stick to blend 3 tbsp. of texture paint with 3 cups of lukewarm water. Accumulate hanging twine and secure flexible halfway. Absorb the finishes of the twine the

paint-water answer for 30 min. Spread out to dry on a plastic garbage bag for 24 hours. Expel flexible and secure external weaving loop.

CHAPTER TWENTY-TWO

PROJECT TWENTY-TWO: NEON MACRAMÉ JARS

That as well as I've been known to purchase food basically because I need the vacant jar a short time later. Should it be that you're in any way similar to me, the present DIY Neon Macramé Jars is an incredible method to put a portion of those jars to utilize. A fun and nautical approach to flavor up your craft stockpiling, neon string includes a summary sprinkle that makes even association something to anticipate.

Materials Needed To Make DIY Neon Macramé Jars

- Neon line

- Empty jars

- Aluminum foil container

- Washi tape

- Scissors

- Exacto blade

- Hot stick firearm

- Measuring tape

Step by step instructions to Make DIY Neon Macramé Jars

Stage 1: Cut five strands of rope each around 6'. Overlap them at the inside and tie an overhand knot; you should now have ten 3' strands of rope. This ought to be all that could be needed for a pickle jar – if your jar is littler/greater alter these lengths in like manner. You can likewise try using fewer strands for littler jars and more strands for greater jars.

Stage 2: If your string will in general conflict once cut, use tape or a lighter to forestall further fraying.

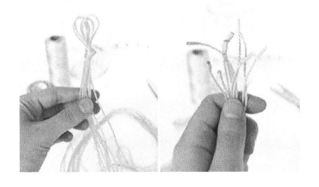

Stage 3: Using your estimating tape, integrate two strands around 2" from the first large knot. Repeat for different strands.

Stage 4: Repeat stage 3, however, separate the joined strands and tie strands from neighboring knots together, additionally around 2" separated, making a net as found in the picture.

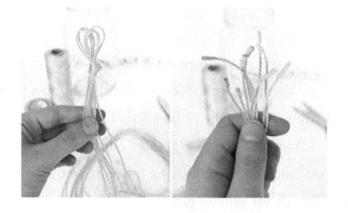

Stage 5: Now and again, it's a smart thought to check how your macramé net is fitting over the jar. If you need to change the way the net looks, essentially loosen the knots you're discontent with and retie at an alternate estimation.

Stage 6: Continue tying knots and watching that it accommodates your jar.

Stage 7: Stop once your macramé net arrives at the mouth of the jar.

Stage 8: On the base of the jar, heated glue the twofold strands of rope onto the jar. It's ideal to do this in the curved region that won't contact the table – this permits the jar to stand level.

Stage 9: Using the exacto blade, remove the enormous unique knot.

Stage 10: Once the huge, unique knot is removed, the jar should stand level on the table. If your rope shreds a ton, utilize extra heated glue to seal the crude edges you simply cut.

Stage 11: At the mouth of the jar, craft glues the string into the strings of the jar.

Stage 12: Use the exacto blade to remove any overabundance line.

Stage 13: As in the past, heated glue any crude edges to forestall fraying.

Stage 14: Measure the boundary of the mouth of the jar and cut a segment of aluminum ½" longer; the width ought to, at any rate, spread the strings of the jar.

Stage 15: If your aluminum strip has raised knocks on it, level them by scouring the handle of your scissors on it too and fro until smooth.

Stage 16: There may even now be some surface when you're set,

yet this adds enthusiasm to the edge!

Stage 17: Use heated glue to make sure about the aluminum strip to the mouth of the jar.

There you have it – repeat on the same number of kinds of jars however you see fit!

CHAPTER TWENTY-THREE

PROJECT TWENTY-THREE: SPECIAL MACRAMÉ WALL HANGING DESIGN

I need to concede that as of not long ago, macramé would have been toward the finish of the rundown of things I needed to hold tight my walls – to me it brought back recollections of mildewed earthy colored pieces I found by the dozen in second-hand shops when I was growing up. One specific macramé find – an owl made out of twine – rings a bell. However, as confirmation that preferences and patterns complete the cycle if just you give them time (I wager that owl is bringing a chunk of change at some hip vintage boutique at present), I've as of late wound up with a desire for this (not really) overlooked craft.

A valid example – my companion Jess as of late purchased the loveliest wall hanging on Etsy (the one you see beneath), complete with flies of neon to loan a pinch of the present-day cool. After I saw it, I was urgent to find out about how these pieces are made – and was so cheerful when a companion consented to give me the once-over. He has worked admirably of bringing macramé out of the twentieth century into the present time and place (ideal for ongoing macramé changes over like me), and I'm excited he chose to give us a look at her – what ends up being entirely convoluted – process. Time to look over your knotting aptitudes!

You Need

Rope

Wooden dowel

Wooden beads

Paintbrush

Scissors

Concealing tape

Paint

May joins the dowel to the wall - she's using removable snares since it's an incredible method to abstain from penetrating openings in the wall.

May cuts the rope up into 14 x 4-yard pieces and 2 x 5-yard pieces. She at that point begins tying the rope in warblers head knots, bookending the dowel with the 5-yard pieces (one on each end)

May proceeds with the remainder of the ropes.

She, at that point, does a twofold half hitch knot.

What's more, proceeds with these right along.

At the point when she gets as far as possible, May begins to tie them slantingly along the ropes

May includes wooden beads to a great extent before tying the knots.

She at that point, starts tying switch knots using four ropes each.

May ties 8 of these.

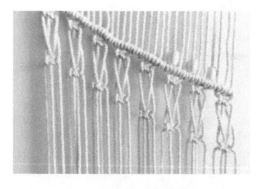

She included a twofold half hitch knot (as in the past).

What's more, brings those along askew.

May includes more beads and carries the knots right to the finishes.

May then trims the finishes of the rope.

She covers off a segment of the closures of the dowel to paint and

include a trace of neon (a lady seeking to win over my affections!)

At last, she includes a fly of watermelon shading to the closures of the ropes.

CHAPTER TWENTY- FOUR

PROJECT TWENTY-FOUR: MACRAMÉ STONE NECKLACE

I love nature, and I particularly love it when I can fuse it into my embellishments. It might be stone or wood beads, a botanical theme, or in the present case: bits of genuine nature as the saint of this DIY stone necklace. I'll tell you the best way to make a basic arrangement of knots to hold a stone (or another fortune), so you can string it on a chain and wear it! I decided to utilize brilliant weaving floss for this DIY stone necklace project, yet any sort of string to suit your style will work! If you incline toward an increasingly unpretentious shading plan, at that point hemp, jute, or cotton string in any shading will likewise function admirably to catch objects like stones.

Supplies expected to make your macramé

Splendidly hued Embroidery Floss

Waterway Rock(s)

4mm Chain – 24-36 inches for every necklace, contingent upon your inclination

6mm Split Rings

Lobster Clasp

Enormous Eye Needle

Scissors

Pincers (you may discover split ring forceps particularly accommodating)

To start with, slice 4 lines to a length of roughly 18 inches. This was a bounty to cover a 2-3 inch stone. If your stone is littler, at that point, you won't need as much length. However, it's in every case better to have an excess of length than insufficient!

Take one line and string on a split ring. (You can substitute a standard hop ring; however, this guarantees it won't sneak off your chain later.) Position the ring in the focal point of the string, and tie it around the other three ropes at their middle point. This will make a focal ring with eight 9-inch strands knotted together at the inside.

Next, pair up two lines that are close to one another. Tie an overhand knot in the two, associating them together, around 1/2 inch from the inside ring in each pair of lines, as appeared previously.

Separate the sets of ropes, and repair them with the neighboring lines. Tie another knot in each pair of ropes around 1/2 inch from

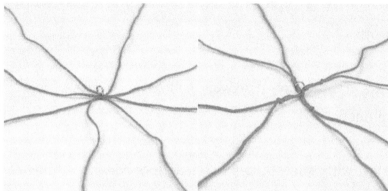

the primary arrangement of knots. You will proceed to separate and substitute the sets, making knots a short good ways from the last arrangement of knots.

Note: if your stone is particularly little, you will need to put the knots nearer to the focal ring, and closer to one another. You're making such a "net" to hold your stone, and the separation

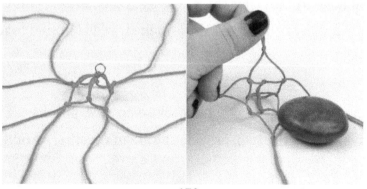

between knots will decide how huge the openings are. Littler stones will require littler openings. You may need to try different things with your stones to discover the separations that work best for you. Take a stab at slipping your stone inside the net as you work, to decide whether your sleeve is a solid match.

At the point when you have made an enormous enough net to hold your stone, slip it inside and tie it firmly around the stone. Here's a tip to get it tight – separate the strings into two sections

and tie them together with how you would tie a shoe. Twofold knot it to get it exceptionally close around the stone. At that point, tie an overhand knot around the twofold knot (which you may likewise call a square knot) to complete it for appearance.

Trim off the finishes to make a tuft, and your DIY stone necklace pendant is finished!

Alternatively, you can light up your chain to coordinate your stone pendant by doing some straightforward weaving. Cut a length of weaving floss that is 6-8 inches longer than your chain. Tie a knot toward one side of the chain, and string the floss onto an enormous eye needle. Weave the floss to and fro through the chain, binds a knot to the opposite finish of the chain to make sure about it.

String your pendant. At that point, associate a ring to one finish of your chain, and a ring and lobster catch to the opposite end to complete your DIY stone necklace.

Remember that you can adjust it to anything hard to penetrate to string another way.

CHAPTER TWENTY- FIVE

PROJECT TWENTY-FIVE: KNOTTED CHEVRON HEADBAND

If you've stacked the same number of bracelets on to your wrists as you can fit, however, aren't prepared to quit knotting, yet this headband is for you. It truly is only an extra-long kinship armband changed to sit perfectly on your head. I picked bright sherbet hues with dim hints, yet if you've at any point taken a gander at a showcase of weaving floss, you realize that the lovely potential blends continue for a long time.

Supplies:

– Embroidery floss (6 hues/12 strands fit my 1/2 inch wide headband)

– Narrow, glossy silk lace – 1/8 to 1/4 inch wide is great

– E6000 or comparative paste that sticks to the plastic

– 1/2 inch wide headband or your inclination

– Coordinated sewing string and needle – discretionary – if you need to sew the knotted piece to the headband for additional strength

My head doesn't suit headbands that tie or versatile into place – I wind up spending the entire day straightening out them – so I utilize plastic. If you like an alternate style, I'm certain you can change this to suit your inclination.

Start by making your extra-long fellowship wristband.

I utilized six strands that are every 10 feet since quite a while ago, collapsed down the middle to be 5 feet in length, yet if your headband is more extensive, your strands may be to be longer.

Bind a removable knot to hold the strands together and work the Classic Chevron Friendship Bracelet (or an example of your decision) until the strip is about 1.5 inches shorter than the length of the headband.

At the point when you're done, unfasten the knot.

Put a spot of paste on the rear of the headband; at that point, begin wrapping the strip once again the headband. Ensure that you cover the strip on the front and back and that if your glossy

silk lace is just single-face that the great side is out. Let this set up for a couple of moments before proceeding.

Trim the tails off of one finish of the knotted strip and paste it down. Once more, let it set up for a couple of moments.

Put some paste on the back and fold the lace over the knotted strip until you've secured everything blemished.

At that point, keep sticking and wrapping, yet behind the knotted strip rather than over it.

Quit sticking and wrapping when you're a similar good way from this end as you were from the other for sticking down the knotted strip.

Trim the tails on this end and paste the entire length of excessively long wristband down, right to the end. You'll most likely need to extend it a little to fit, and which is acceptable. (Possibly stick the end if you would like to line over the back to make sure about the knotted piece.)

Keep sticking on the back and fold around the finish of the strip until you arrive at the finish of the headband, flawlessly sticking the finish of the lace on the back.

Now, if you just stuck the end, you can fasten to and fro over the back, getting the edges of the knotted piece and pulling it firmly into the right spot. This is a decent decision of the strip that has conflicting edges.

CHAPTER TWENTY- SIX

PROJECT TWENTY-SIX: MACRAMÉ BEADED BAREFOOT SANDALS

Shoeless sandals are incredible for strolling around the seashore or on the grass in summer. They can even be worn with flip flounders that have a toe post as well. If you extravagant creation a couple of these, follow my simple instructional exercise underneath.

As a matter of first importance, accumulate your materials!

100% cotton yarn in pale pink or your preferred shade. You can likewise utilize macramé string – see various sorts here.

20 to 30 silver-tone round beads with huge gaps, for example, silver spacer globules.

Bulldog cuts.

Scissors.

Stage 1 – Trimming the yarn

Cut three long segments of yarn around 3m long. The yarn should belong, to represent the lower leg straps later. At that point, discover the approx. The midpoint of those three strips and tie a

knot, as appeared in the image above.

Stage 2 – Braiding the toe circle

On one side of the knot, mesh a few creeps of the strands together.

Stage 3: The toe circle

At that point, fix the knot you made before and retie it after making a circle with the meshed strand. This will frame the toe circle for your shoe!

Stage 4: Making a macramé square knot

The principal part of the shoe that will go down from your lower leg, over the front of your foot to the toe, is shaped using macramé knotting. You'll have six strands to work with currently, so independent them into three strands, each with two strands in. Beginning the correct hand side, place that strand over the center one, as appeared above, making a D-formed circle.

Stage 5: Macramé square knot

At that point, take the left strand and string that one under the center stand and into the D-molded circle.

Stage 6: Macramé square knot proceeded

At that point, pull both of the left and right strands to make the initial segment of the square knot. See pic above for how it should see this stage!

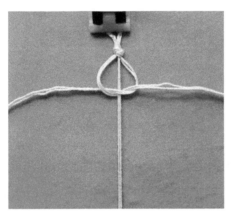

Stage 7: Macramé square knot proceeded

Repeat the procedure on the left-hand side. Spot the left strand over the middle strand; at that point, string the correct strand under the inside strand and into the (regressive) D-molded circle you've recently made.

Stage 8 – Macramé square knot proceeded

Pull both the left and right strands from the center remain to finish your first complete macramé square knot.

Stage 9 – Making a macramé square knot with beads

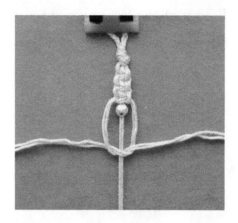

Make another two square knots, with the goal that you have three knots altogether and afterwards string on one of your silver round beads onto the center strand. Make the initial segment of your next square knot around this globule. The procedure is equivalent to previously, see the photograph above!

Stage 10 – Macramé knotting with beads

Complete the macramé square knot simply like the others.

Stage 11 – Making a macramé beaded strand

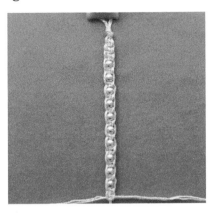

Repeat stages 10 and 11 until you have ten beads altogether, joined to the center strand using macramé square knots. (Coincidentally, my feet are a UK size 5, which is US size seven and European 38. If your feet are greater, you may need to utilize a couple more globules for this part.)

Stage 12 – Braiding the lower leg straps

Finish the beaded area by doing a couple of plain square knots without beads and afterwards split the strands into two (each will

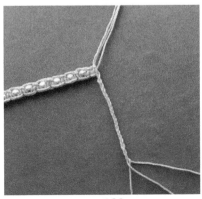

have three strings). Mesh those to make the lower leg straps, until they arrive at a length of at any rate 50cm. This will guarantee you can fold them over your lower leg a few times!

You can complete the straps by just knotting them or include another silver bead toward the end in the middle of a square knot for a touch of embellishment. In case you will do this, make a point to tie a twofold knot at the base of the last square knot to make sure about it into place. Trim any abundance string and afterwards repeat stages 1 to 12 to make your subsequent shoe!